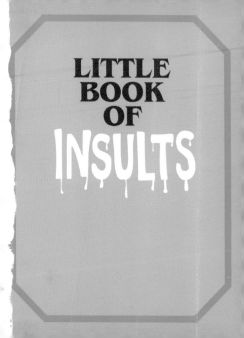

LITTLE
BOOK
OF
INSULTS

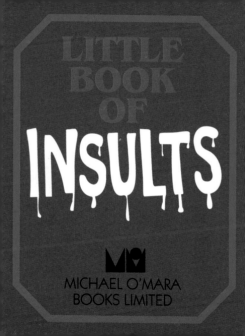

LITTLE
BOOK
OF
INSULTS

MICHAEL O'MARA
BOOKS LIMITED

First published in Great Britain in 1995 by
Michael O'Mara Books Limited
9 Lion Yard
Tremadoc Road
London SW4 7NQ

A CIP catalogue record for this book is available from
the British Library

ISBN 1-85479-798-0

1 3 5 7 9 10 8 6 4 2

Designed by Robert Updegraff

Printed and bound in Singapore

*H*e reminds me of nothing so much as a dead fish before it has time to stiffen.

**George Orwell
of Clement Attlee**

Overweight, overbosomed, overpaid and under-talented, she set the acting profession back a decade.

**David Susskind
on Elizabeth Taylor in
*Cleopatra***

*T*ories are always wrong,
but they are always wrong
at the right moment.

Lady Violet Bonham Carter

*T*aut and tight-lipped mistress of the baseline, she is the all-American golden girl become the champion of monotony.

**Paul West
on Chris Evert**

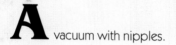

A vacuum with nipples.

**Otto Preminger
on Marilyn Monroe**

*S*o boring you fell asleep halfway through her name.

**Alan Bennett
on Arianna Stassinopoulos**

He is the only genius with an IQ of 60.

**Gore Vidal
on Andy Warhol**

*B*oy George is all England needs - another queen who can't dress.

**Joan Rivers
on Boy George**

If you say, 'Hiya, Clark, how are you?' he's stuck for an answer.

**Ava Gardener
on Clark Gable**

*H*e is going round
the country stirring up
apathy.

**William Whitelaw
on Harold Wilson**

Simply a radio
personality who outlived
his prime . . .

**Evelyn Waugh
on Winston Churchill**

*A*void all needle drugs
- the only dope worth
shooting is Richard Nixon.

**Abbie Hoffman
on the former President of
the United States**

English Literature's
performing flea.

**Sean O'Casey
on P.G. Wodehouse**

It was wonderful to find America, but it would have been more wonderful to miss it.

Mark Twain

*N*o-one ever went broke underestimating the taste of the American public.

H. L. Mencken

*S*hit floats.

**Nikita Khrushchev
(on Brezhnev's rise to the top)**

George Bush has a much more visible absence than Ronald Reagan.

Lance Morrow

*T*he great thing about
Errol was that you knew
precisely where you were
with him - because he
always let you down.

**David Niven
on Errol Flynn**

You always knew
where you were with
Goldwyn. Nowhere.

**F.Scott Fitzgerald
on Samuel Goldwyn**

*F*rance is a dog-hole.

William Shakespeare, *All's Well That Ends Well*

A face unclouded
by thought.

**Lillian Hellman
on Norma Shearer**

****!

*I*t is absurd to say that there are neither ruins nor curiosities in America when they have their mothers and their manners.

Oscar Wilde

You can't see as well as these fucking flowers - and they're fucking plastic.

**John McEnroe
to a line judge**

*N*owadays, a parlour maid as ignorant as Queen Victoria was when she came to the throne, would be classed as mentally defective.

Bernard Shaw

Mr Gladstone speaks to me as if I were a public meeting.

Queen Victoria

****!

A sheep in sheep's clothing.

**Winston Churchill
on Clement Attlee**

The best time I ever had with Joan Crawford was when I pushed her down the stairs in *Whatever Happened to Baby Jane.*

Bette Davis

Every word she writes is a lie, including *and* and *the*.

Mary McCarthy on Lillian Hellman

$\mathcal{S}$he's the best man in England.

**Ronald Reagan
on Margaret Thatcher**

****!

*C*auliflower is nothing
but cabbage with a
college education.

Mark Twain

She was a devout Christian Scientist, but not a good one. She kept confusing herself with God.

**Mrs Gordon Smith
on Lady Astor**

Heaven for climate;
Hell for society.

Mark Twain

. . . bad mannered little
shits.

Noel Coward on The Beatles

*W*alter Mondale has all the charisma of a speed bump.

**Will Durst
on Walter F. Mondale**

* * * * !

*S*he was good at playing abstract confusion in the same way that a midget is good at being short.

**Clive James
on Marilyn Monroe**

Life is too short to learn German.

Richard Porson

I am free of prejudices. I hate everyone equally.

W. C. Fields

I wouldn't say she was open-minded on the Middle East so much as empty-headed. For instance, she probably thinks that Sinai is the plural of sinuses.

**Jonathan Aitken
on Margaret Thatcher**

Small, short-sighted, blond, barbed - she reminds me of a bright little hedgehog.

**Edwina Currie
on Teresa Gorman**

****!

She has done for our party what King Herod did for babysitting.

**Andrew Mackay
on Edwina Currie**

Those who scream and throw eggs are not the real unemployed. If they were really hard up, they would be eating them.

**Norman Tebbit
to a journalist**

H

e looks like a
refugee from his sunlamp.

**John Major
on Robert Kilroy Silk**

*A*lways forgive your enemies, but never forget their names.

Robert Kennedy

H

e has crawled so far up the backside of NATO that you can't see the soles of his feet.

Ken Livingstone
on Gerald Kaufman

A great actress from the waist down.

**Dame Margaret Kendal
on Sarah Bernhardt**

A little bit of a squirt.

Harry S. Truman on Joseph Stalin

...a tub of old guts.

Ezra Pound on Gertrude Stein

*S*he's one of the few actresses in Hollywood history who looks more animated in still photographs than she does on the screen.

**Michael Medved
on Raquel Welch**

*S*helley should not be read, but inhaled through a gas pipe.

Lionel Trilling
on Percy Bysshe Shelley

He looks like the guy in the science fiction movie who is the first to see 'the Creature.'

**David Frye
on Gerald Ford**

The Greeks - dirty and impoverished descendants of a bunch of la-de-da fruit salads who invented democracy and then forgot how to use it while walking around dressed up like girls.

P.J. O'Rourke

Too bad all the people who know how to run the country are busy driving cabs and cutting hair.

George Burns

$\mathcal{M}$aybe it's the
hair. Maybe it's the teeth.
Maybe it's the intellect.
No, it's the hair.

Tom Shales
on Farrah Fawcett

A sort of friendship recognized by the police.

**Robert Louis Stevenson
on marriage**

I f Kitchener was not a great man, he was, at least, a great poster.

Margot Asquith

The English have no exalted sentiments. They can all be bought.

Napoleon Bonaparte

I am willing to love all mankind, except an American.

Samuel Johnson

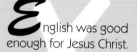

*E*nglish was good
enough for Jesus Christ.

**Ralph Melnyk
on bilingualism**

The most notorious
whore in all the world.

**Peter Wentworth
on Mary, Queen of Scots**

France is a country
where the money falls
apart in your hands and
you can't tear the toilet
paper.

Billy Wilder

Advertising is the rattling of a stick inside a swill bucket.

George Orwell

$\mathcal{A}$uthors are easy to get on with - if you're fond of children.

Michael Joseph, publisher